SURVIVAL GUIDE TO PARTIES

Also published by Collins

Survival Guide to School
Survival Guide to Friends
by Brough Girling

Survival Guide to Parents
Survival Guide to Pets
Survival Guide to Food
by Scoular Anderson

SURVIVAL GUIDE TO PARTIES

Includes new, improved traditional party games!

Brough Girling

Illustrated by Judy Brown

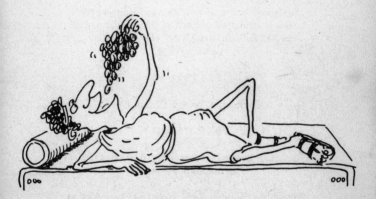

Collins
An Imprint of HarperCollinsPublishers

First published in Great Britain by Collins in 1995
Collins is an imprint of HarperCollins*Publishers* Ltd.,
77-85 Fulham Palace Road, Hammersmith,
London W6 8JB

13 5 7 9 8 6 4 2

Copyright © Brough Girling 1995

ISBN 0 00 675042 7

The author asserts the moral right to be identified as
the author of the work.

Printed and bound in Great Britain by HarperCollins
Manufacturing Ltd, Glasgow.

CONTENTS

AUTHOR'S FOREWORD
– AND SPECIAL WARNING

IF YOU THINK THAT PARTIES ARE FOR FUN – THINK AGAIN. Parties are as dangerous as a tiger with a toothache. At a party that goes wrong you can lose friends, possessions, dignity and self-esteem, *and* 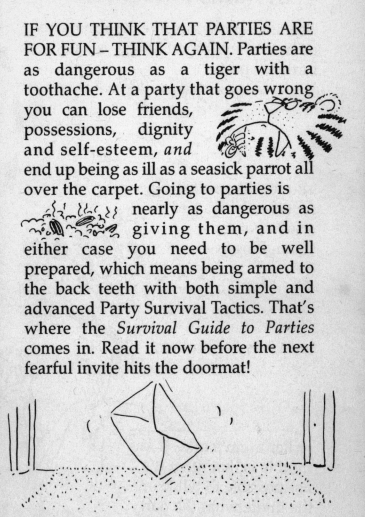 end up being as ill as a seasick parrot all over the carpet. Going to parties is nearly as dangerous as giving them, and in either case you need to be well prepared, which means being armed to the back teeth with both simple and advanced Party Survival Tactics. That's where the *Survival Guide to Parties* comes in. Read it now before the next fearful invite hits the doormat!

OK, BUT WHAT SORT OF PARTY WILL IT BE?

The invitation hits the doormat. You open it: 'Hey! Karen Bloggs is having a birthday party!'

You feel like accepting (you've always had a soft spot for Karen Bloggs –

or maybe her brother,

or her mum's cakes). The trouble is that often it's not possible to tell from the invite what the party will be like. A sure way to get some idea is to consult your

HOROSCOPE GUIDE TO BIRTHDAY PARTIES

It's obvious when you think about it. Because people have birthday parties on their birthdays, it's very simple to work out what their star sign is, and then to use their horoscope to predict what sort of party they are likely to have.

Next time you get an invite look up the date on these pages of your *Survival Guide to Parties*, and check the gig out! (But see also SURVIVAL GUIDE TO PARTY INVITES page 18.)

ARIES March 21-April 19

This is the sign of the ram — but beware, it doesn't mean Ariens have sheepish birthday parties! When they're not lying down eating bits of grass, rams run round butting people and crashing through other people's hedges, and that's a clue to what sort of party it may be; lots of charging around, butting in on people's private conversations, and as much grass and hay as you can eat! Not recommended.

TAURUS April 20-May 20

Beware of the bull! Taureans are just like Ariens (see above) only much worse! (And don't go in your best, new *red* party frock — especially if you're a boy.) You have been warned...

GEMINI May 21-June 20
Simple! Gemini is
the sign of twins —
so watch out, there
may be two of them!
This is bad news,
because it means
you have to take
two presents, and
there's absolutely no
guarantee that their
birthday party will be twice
as good as anyone else's! Best avoided.

CANCER June 21-July 22
The sign of the crab,
so watch out for
fishpaste sandwiches!
You are also likely
to get nipped on the
bum by a large pair
of vicious pincers.
People at these parties
are generally crabby, and there's a
smell not unlike a box of week-old
kippers. Try to think of something
else to go to that day.

LEO July 23-August 22
Really dangerous!
These party-givers
think they are lions.
There'll be lots of
raw red meat
to eat, and some
really rough games. After tea (often
antelope or wildebeest) they just lie
round under trees swishing their
tails and growling gently at anyone
who mildly suggests doing anything
else. Make sure you take a really
impressive present, as befits a king
of the jungle.

VIRGO August 23-September 22
By nature these
kids are real little
fusspots. They're
the sort of children
who take their
shoes off inside
*without being told
to*... So the food will
be arranged neatly on the plates and
if you're lucky enough to play outside
there'll be polythene sheets spread
out on the lawn. Think of an excuse,
quickly.

LIBRA September 23-October 22
These kids are pretty wierd too. They think they are a pair of scales. They're dead keen on balance and fairness, so if they think your present for them isn't good enough you'll probably have to stay out in the kitchen while everyone who brought decent pressies tucks in to tea. If you win a prize they make you share it out again. On balance, don't bother...

SCORPIO October 23-November 21
The sign of the scorpion. Understand? They are even more dangerous than Leos because they are small and look quite harmless (repellent, but harmless). But they always get you in the end. For instance, you win first prize in their best party game, and when you leave to go home they make you give it back. The sting is always in the tail. Stay at home that day...

SAGITTARIUS November 22-December 21

Watch out! This is the star sign of someone who's half horse and half archer, so at the party if they don't buck you off and trample you to death with their clumsy great feet, they'll fill you as full as a porcupine with arrows! And do you really want raw carrots and sugar lumps for tea?

CAPRICORN December 22-January 19

As this is the sign of the goat, their parties are very similar to ones given by Ariens (see page 10). If anything, the charging round and butting is worse, and so is the food. Goats are famous for eating things like cardboard boxes and old socks, and for breaking out

into other people's gardens and destroying the roses. You'd be better off staying at home with a good book... like this one!

Simple. If you think that no party is complete without lemonade, orange juice, Coke, Pepsi, Tango, or even the very latest diet, caffeine-free, low alcohol, environmentally friendly fizzy drink, forget it! These children are born under the sign of the water carrier (whatever that is). So all you get to wash down their rather boring sandwiches is, you've guessed it, WATER!

PISCES February 19-March 20

Which brings us to dreaded Pisces, the sign of the fish. The party often features games in their outdoor swimming pool – in March! And the food will be large quantities of dried ants' eggs and bits of flaky stuff that look like something that's come out of the turn-ups of your dad's oldest pair of trousers. At least there'll be plenty to drink...

So if you believe in astrology, the answer's simple – don't go to parties!

SURVIVAL GUIDE

TO PARTY INVITES!

Before taking the brave step of accepting an invitation to a party, you need some idea of what sort of party it's likely to be! After all, it's your fault if you say Yes to something that turns out to be about as much fun as standing on your head in a puddle of mud for the afternoon. A sure way to stay safe is to use the horoscope guide on page 9, but you can often also tell a lot from the wording of the invitation.

For example:

Darling Chummykins,
Please come to my partypoo! There's going to be oodles and oodles of fabbydabby foods for you to fill your scrummy tummykins with, and lots and lots of lovely games !!! How soopa !!!

This party will almost certainly turn out to be as soppy as the Christmas Fairy's powder puff. Don't go.

FAIRY POWDER

Hi Guys, I'm having a gig. Mosey on round and check it out. See ya, kid.

This child thinks it comes from New York's street scene, or has been watching too much television. Unless you too think that happiness is carrying a handgun and wearing a baseball cap back to front, forget it.

Hello!

I'm having a little party in the woods. We will dally among the daffydowndillies and dance among the daisies with dewdrops in our hair. We will slide down thistle stems, and gather garlands of golden dandelions to herald the summer's sun.

Please come.

This invitation has come from a Flower Fairy. On no account accept, you'd hate it (unless, of course you're a Flower Fairy).

This invitation has come from a Rottweiler, or possibly a Bengal tiger (see page 45). Don't go.

Jo is having a party on Friday 19th September at 4 o'clock. There'll be lots of food and drink and plenty of games (including computer games!) Do come and have some fun!

This invitation sounds inviting – accept!

TO BALLOONS ON THE GATE

As anyone who has ever been to anything like any sort of party knows, the usual way of announcing that the party is *here*, and of guiding all those eager little present-bearing guests to your house for the big event, is to tie a few balloons to your front gate.

PATHETIC! That's no way to herald to the world the venue of the party of the year, of the decade, of the century!

SURVIVAL TIP: What you need to do is to rig up something much more lavish, preferably in neon with flashing lights and arrows, like this:

A constant fanfare of trumpets, and a dazzling display of fireworks may also be helpful to create the right effect and welcome.

ANOTHER SPECIAL SURVIVAL TIP:

There may be times when you are asked to someone else's party and you don't want too many other people to go to it – for instance, if you have a hunch that the food is going to be particularly mega-delicious, or you are madly in love with the person giving the party! (Or would like to be.) *The survival tactic here is quite simple;* arrive nice and early for the party and move the balloons from the front gate of the party house to *another* house, in another street or even another town (for added laughs you could tie them to the front door of the local police station, dentist, or undertaker).

That way you should have the party to yourself!

THE TRUTH ABOUT
BALLOONS!

There are parents around who will say daft things like: 'All we'll need for a party is a few nice balloons.'

Nonsense! Balloons are just thin pieces of flexible skin full of air – just like teachers!

And like teachers they are not much fun, they are not useful, and they are not edible. Why are we supposed to get so excited about balloons? If they don't burst on the way home from the party, you keep them, and the next day they're as wrinkly as your granny (but without the happy, smiling face and the chocolate biscuits!)

SURVIVAL TIP: Forget about balloons, they're boring!

SURVIVAL GUIDE

TO PERILOUS PARTY PARENTS

THE THREE Ps.
A party is only as good as the parents of the person whose party it is, OK? Most hopeless parties are therefore the fault of the parents (hence the useful party expression, 'I blame the parents'.)

In order to avoid the danger of going to a party that's going to be a complete floppo, you therefore need to be able to identify Perilous Party Parents (the three Ps). In this section of your Survival Guide we introduce you to a few of the most common, and dangerous species, so that if you get an invite from them you can suddenly remember that you've already got a date that afternoon for an important disco in Rio de Janeiro.

COMMON NAME:
HEARTY PARTY PARENTS

Latin Name: *Slappus Backus*

Common Calls: These parents are easily identified by their common calls. They are inclined to say really embarrassing things like: 'I say! My word! Who's a pretty little girl then? And what a lovely party frock!' OR, if you're a boy: 'Come along in then young fella-me-lad! Get stuck into the grub! There's lots more where that came from! Ho-Ho-Ho!'

Appearance: Hearty Party Dads often wear terrible waistcoats, and may even smoke a pipe! They always wear large grins, as do Hearty Party Mums who often have sticky-out teeth and hideous laughs. It's not unknown for mums like this to wear shell suits at their children's parties.

Other Characteristics: The main identifying behaviour of Hearty Party Parents is that they are unbelievably jolly all the time.

Habitat: About halfway through their child's party you'll often find them in the kitchen gathered round a bottle of gin, and laughing particularly loudly at their own jokes.

COMMON NAME: PARTY POOPERS
Latin Name: *Grimus Grimus*

Common Calls: These are the most miserable parents it's possible to have. They don't really want their kids to have a party, and the only reason they know for having one is to pay back all the people who have given parties for their children. Their common call, therefore, is something like: 'I suppose we'll have to have a party,' or, 'It's only fair,' or 'You can all watch television, so long as it's only *Blue Peter*'.

Appearance: They have pale faces and black or grey clothes, and their mouths turn down at the corners.

Other Characteristics: Avoid parties given by these people at all costs. The food will be jam sandwiches with the crusts left on, and perhaps an apple if you're *really* lucky! Anything as wacky as Coke or Pepsi is right out! Goody-bags are out too – the best you can hope to come away with is a lousy pencil but definitely with no little eraser on the top.

COMMON NAME: PARENTS WHO JOIN IN

Latin Name: *Alltogethernowus*

Common Calls: These parents have the strange idea that they are actually part of the party, not just the providers of the food, drink and prizes. They are therefore inclined to say daft things like: 'All right, guys and gals, let's get stuck in then shall we?' or 'Hi, folks! Fancy a game of Sardines or Hide and Seek?'

Appearance: You can easily tell the dads by their clothes. They wear horrible sleeveless jerseys with lots of squiggly patterns on them – like a colour TV that's on the blink. They often have corduroy trousers and sometimes even beards. The mums wear sloppy jumpers and smile a lot. (Generally they are not as dangerous as the dads.)

COMMON NAME: JIM NASTIES

Latin Name: *Pater cum Adidas*
Common Calls: 'Ready! Steady! GO!' and 'Faster child! Faster!'

Distinguishing Characteristics: Jim Nasties are *always* men, i.e. dads.

They seem to think that a children's party should be rather like the Olympic Games. They organise competitions, and even *races*! Help! The whole thing is more like a really bad games lesson in a school gym than a party.

Appearance: Simple; these dads appear at their own children's parties dressed in track suits! Really serious cases wear a whistle round their neck on a stupid bit of ribbon. Honestly…

COMMON NAME:
MR AND MRS MONEYBAGS

Latin Name: *Lotta Loota*

Common Calls: You'd think that parents with lots of money would be rather good at throwing parties, but you'd be wrong. You can tell what they're inclined to be like from their common calls: 'Oi! Keep that football away from the Rolls!' 'Come in, but take your shoes off – this carpet cost a hundred quid a square millimetre.' 'Don't put your fingers on the wallpaper – it's made of real suede.'

Appearance: These parents glitter. The mums have so much jewellery on that they rattle when they walk, and at Christmas parties you can easily confuse them with the tree. The dads have gold rings too, and gold medallions, and even gold teeth.

SURVIVAL GUIDE

TO FANCY DRESS

There are few situations more terribly dangerous than fancy-dress parties! If you don't give the whole thing a lot of careful thought you can end up being as popular as Mr Hitler the Traffic Warden.

The main problem with fancy-dress parties is YOUR COSTUME.

First, *the Golden Rule for fancy-dress parties:* **DO NOT TRY TO GO AS KERMIT THE FROG!**
Reasons:

1. Everyone else will go as Kermit the Frog.

2. You will not look like Kermit the Frog – you will look like a heap of green string that the dog's been chewing. And anyway you're much too big.

3. You will not sound like Kermit the Frog, who sounds like an American cat with its tail in a mincer.

SPECIAL NOTE: *Look, if you are a small green American person who sounds like a cat with its tail in a mincer, OK, go as Kermit the Frog. If not, don't say I didn't warn you.*

ANOTHER SPECIAL NOTE:
Everything we've said so far about Kermit the Frog also applies to Miss Piggy.

IT'S ALSO RATHER IMPORTANT NOT TO GO AS EITHER **A WITCH OR A PIRATE**. Not only will there be millions of witches and pirates who all look a lot better than you, but witches' long fingernail thingies make it difficult to eat the food, and it's almost impossible when wearing a pirate's eyepatch and trying to drink without missing most of your mouth completely!

Here are some other things 'not to go as' to fancy-dress parties:

THE SURVIVAL GUIDE TO FANCY-DRESS PARTIES
NOT TO GO AS LIST

Captain Scarlet

Batman (or Robin)

**Any Ninja Turtle
(too old-fashioned)**

Any animal

Any footballer/ballet dancer

Mother Teresa of Calcutta

Joan of Ark

Madonna (Yuk)

Any Muppet (see page 35)

FANCY DRESS – THE SURVIVAL GUIDE SECRET OF SUCCESS

Here, for your eyes only, is the secret of success for all fancy-dress situations:

First,
KEEP IT SIMPLE!

Second,
KEEP THEM GUESSING!

For example, as you probably know by now, if you spend about three and a half weeks getting dressed up to look like the Lion King you walk in at the fancy-dress party and everyone says: 'What are you supposed to be?'
You: 'The Lion King'

Them: 'Well, you don't look like the Lion King. You look like a hearth rug that the cat's been ill on!'
And home you go in your mum's car and a flood of tears.

WHAT YOU SHOULD HAVE DONE:
If you'd kept it simple you could have painted your face red (mum's red lipstick), worn an orange T-shirt and a pair of green trousers (preparation time about 3.5 minutes). You arrive at the party, they start guessing:

Them: 'What are you supposed to be?'
You: 'A traffic light, stupid.'
Them: 'Wow! How brilliant! How witty and amusing! And so simple! You're my hero/heroine! Can I have your autograph? Wow! Swoon swoon! Marry me or I die!'
See?

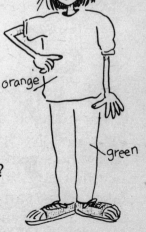

'What are you supposed to be? Julius Caesar?'

'No, dumbo, a snowdrift!'

Or here's another one: Paint yourself green. Blow up about twenty purple balloons and stick them all over you. What are you now?

A BUNCH OF GRAPES, OF COURSE!

SPECIAL SURVIVAL TACTIC:

Don't go as a bunch of grapes if you're one of those unpleasant children who likes to join in games in order to win them. The balloons get in the way and the chances of picking up any major prizes are therefore slim. If, however, you like to get out of games and competitions, the bunch of grapes ploy could be just the thing for you!

SURVIVAL GUIDE

TO TRADITIONAL PARTY GAMES—BUT NEW AND IMPROVED!

You'll only survive a party of your own if you get the games right. And if you've got parents who are anything at all like Party Poopers (see page 29) they're quite likely to say that 'traditional old party games are best'. They'll think that things like Hunt the Thimble, Pass the Parcel, Pin the Tail on the Donkey and Musical Chairs are the greatest fun since man first slipped on a banana skin.

Well they're wrong. These corny old games are about as enjoyable as a long trip to the dentist.

Here, in this particularly useful section of your *Survival Guide to Parties*, are new and improved versions of these games. If you use one or two of these at any party you organise, everyone will agree that your party was the most memorable one of the year!

PASS THE PYTHON!

In this upgraded version of the boring old game there's no need for all that stupid paper and silly string! All you do is sit your guests in a big circle, and give them a really large, bad-tempered python (about two metres long is fine). They have to pass the python round the circle while you play some tinkling, soppy music.

When the music stops, the children holding the python must stop, and the kid holding its head will almost certainly be eaten alive. Keep playing until only one child, and the now even larger python, are left. That child is the winner (and the python didn't do too badly either!)

MUSICAL CHORES

This is an excellent game for anyone organising a party. You know how your mum or dad are always saying 'Tidy your room', 'Make your bed', 'Clean your bike', 'Cut the grass', 'Empty the rubbish', 'Dry the dishes', 'Fetch the shopping', 'Walk the dog', 'Clean out your gerbils,' etc. etc.?

Well, a great survival tactic is to use a party to get these chores done! All you do is give one of these chores to each guest or player. The child that does their chore most thoroughly is the winner. While they are doing them you sit in a large armchair by the fire listening to your favourite music – that's why this splendid game is called Musical Chores!

HUNT THE BENGAL TIGER!

Let's face it – any sissy little kid can hunt a thimble! But what good is a silly thimble to the street-cred, worldly-wise, trainers-and-jeans kids of today?

Jazz the old game up a bit by replacing the thimble with a fully grown Bengal tiger. All you do is hide the tiger somewhere round the house or garden (the airing cupboard is quite a good place, or dad's toolshed, or even the boot of the car). The clever bit is that you tell the players that they are looking for a thimble. You'll soon tell from the screams that the tiger has been found, and the bloodstains should lead you to the winner!

(Actually, the Bengal tiger usually wins this game.)

PUTTING THE TAIL ON THE PIRANHA!

This is not all that dissimilar from Hunt the Bengal tiger – and is just as much fun (and as messy!). Forget the dumb old picture of a donkey, and get a really large aquarium full of piranha fish and make sure that they haven't had a good meal for several weeks.

Then cut out the shape of a fish-tail from a piece of cardboard like this:

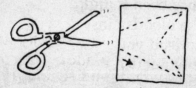

To play the game your guests take it in turns to put their hands in the fish tank and try to stick the cardboard tail on any one of the piranhas. Just listen to their squeals of delight as the tank becomes a frothing red mass of food-frenzied man-eating fish!

The winner is the child who, at the end of the game, has the most fingers left.

SURVIVAL TIP: You can jolly the game up even more by adding a couple of crocodiles! (And it's a good idea to include plenty of boxes of sticking plasters in the prizes for this game.)

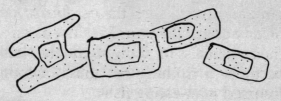

SURVIVING AT CHRISTMAS !

The main difficulty about parties at Christmas is that there aren't any! Yes, lots of aunts and uncles and cousins, etc., come round, but then all the adults want to do is watch the TV! They sit round the set watching *'Mary Poppins'* or *'Those Magnificent Men in Their Flying Machines'* or *'The Sound of Music'* while your gran and grandad complain that in their day they used to make their own entertainment! (And your dad falls asleep.)

Well you can do something about this! Tell them to turn the telly off and you will perform your very own

CHRISTMAS PARTY PANTOMIME !

All you need is four actors – it doesn't matter if they are boys or girls – in pantomime no one cares!

MAKE YOUR OWN PANTOMIME: CINDERELLA
CAST:

CINDERELLA

AN UGLY SISTER

BUTTONS

FAIRY GODMOTHER
(who also plays Prince Charming)

ACT ONE (There is only one act)
Scene One

CINDERS: Oh dear, here I sit in the cinders like a fag-end in an ashtray. I've only got Buttons as a friend. We're so poor I've even only got *one* ugly sister. Sob Sob.
Enter BUTTONS: Cheer up, Cinders. Prince Charming is having one of his balls up at the palace.

CINDERS: I won't be able to go. My Ugly Sister will go and marry the prince and live happily ever after.
BUTTONS: No, Cinders, I have your invite here. (*He holds up a large white envelope.*)

Enter UGLY SISTER: I'll take that, thank you, Buttons. (*She snatches it.*)
BUTTONS: Hey!

SISTER: Shut up, Buttons, or we'll replace you with a zip! I shall go to the ball and marry the prince. My looks will enchant him. I've got lips like petals...

BUTTONS: Yes, bicycle petals.

SISTER: And black hair...

BUTTONS: Yes, it matches your teeth.

SISTER: And it shines...

BUTTONS: Like your nose!

CINDERS: Oh, you are fly, Buttons!

SISTER: I'm going to fix my make-up. (*Exit.*)

BUTTONS: (*shouting after her*): I'll phone Ready-Mix Concrete!

Enter FAIRY GODMOTHER: Don't fret, Cinders. I'm your Fairy Godmother. You *shall* go to the ball.

CINDERS: How?

GODMOTHER: Buttons, go and get a huge pumpkin and six white mice.

BUTTONS: OK.

GODMOTHER: And while he's doing that we'll go to the ball. If we hurry we'll get the 14A bus.

BUTTONS: Hey! What about the pumpkin and the mice?

GODMOTHER: What about them? Who do you think I am, Paul blooming Daniels? (*She and Cinders leave.*)

BUTTONS (*to audience*):
Our scene we now are shiftin',
Off to the palace
And out of this kitchin'!

Scene Two

PRINCE CHARMING: I'm Prince Charming.
Rich. Handsome. Modest!

Enter CINDERS, UGLY SISTER AND
BUTTONS.

UGLY SISTER: That prince is the man for
me! (*She approaches him, but he speaks to
Cinderella.*)
PRINCE: You can have the honour of
dancing with me!
CINDERS: Oh good. (*she slips her shoes off.*)

SISTER: (*she kicks off her very large shoes.*) Come on, Buttons. Dance with me, and steer me near to his royal highness-ship.
They dance.

PRINCE: I have an announcement to make. I shall marry the girl whose foot fits this crystal slipper. (*He picks up one of the Ugly Sister's shoes*) Every girl in the kingdom must try it on.
SISTER: I've been trying it on all evening!
PRINCE (*to Sister*): See if your foot fits the crystal slipper.
BUTTONS: Her foot wouldn't fit the Crystal Palace!!
PRINCE: Oh no! It fits!
SISTER: Great. Let's get married!

CINDERS: *(to audience)*
Although I thought the Prince was
charming,
I'm glad my sister's foot did fit.
Though he's rich and quite good
looking,
He really is a total twit,
And she is mutton dressed as mutton –
I'll play safe and marry Buttons!

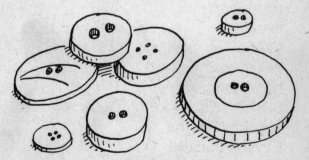

THE END

SURVIVAL GUIDE

TO PARTY PROVERBS

A PLATE OF MARMITE
SANDWICHES DOES NOT
A PARTY MAKE.

BALLOONS ARE FOR WIMPS.

DON'T COUNT YOUR PRESENTS UNTIL THEY'RE UNWRAPPED.

PEOPLE IN GLASSHOUSES SHOULDN'T THROW PARTIES.

HE WHO STICKS JELLY AND CUSTARD IN HIS EARS WILL FIND HIMSELF A TRIFLE DEAF.

NEVER START A PARTY YOU CAN'T FINISH.

GLORIA SLOPBUCKET'S PARTICULARLY VICIOUS PRACTICAL JOKES!

You may or may not have come across Gloria Slopbucket before – she's Britain's hardest-hitting agony aunt. She is also an authority on Particularly Vicious Practical Jokes. As she says herself: *'What's the point of having a party if you can't invite your best friends and have a good laugh at their expense!'*

So, here is a selection of her more inventive (and humiliating) practical jokes.

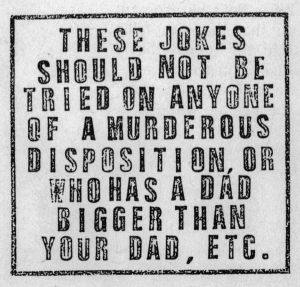

THESE JOKES SHOULD NOT BE TRIED ON ANYONE OF A MURDEROUS DISPOSITION, OR WHO HAS A DAD BIGGER THAN YOUR DAD, ETC.

*'Hi there, little jokesters! Here to really make your party go with a swing is my first vicious practical joke. It's called Custard down the Trousers.'**

CUSTARD DOWN THE TROUSERS

Put a large funnel down the front of someone's trousers. Tell them that you are going to put a pound coin on their forehead and that they have got to bring their head down so that the coin falls into the funnel that's tucked in their waistband. They will look at the ceiling while you balance the coin on their forehead.

*It needs to be pointed out that in this joke, the custard actually goes down the *inside* of the trousers – this is no simple 'Let's dry your trousers with a cloth' job. Dry cleaning could well be involved.

While they are looking at the ceiling you swiftly pour a large bucket of cold custard into the funnel. Then run for it.

'Now here's another.'

EGG NUTTING

Challenge a friend to an Egg Nutting contest (for this little joke you need an accomplice).

Egg nutting sounds simple. Two of you sit opposite each other on chairs with a teaspoon in your mouths. You explain to your challenger that you will take it in turns to try to use the spoon to bash each other on the head (holding it in your mouth). I'll tell you now that this is almost impossible to do – all you can manage is a tiny little tap.

Let them go first. They won't manage to give you much of a bash. When it's your turn, however, you use your accomplice who stands behind your challenger's chair, and taps them smartly on the nut with a teaspoon. This will make your challenger try even harder, but with no better result.

How your friends will roar with laughter as they see what's going on! And how your challenger will roar with rage when he works it out, too!
'What fun! Now for…'

BOAT RACE

In this particularly vicious trick you tell two friends that they are going to have a special boat race. You place a metal tray full of water on the floor in front of them. Their 'boats' will be matchsticks, and all they have to do is blow their stick to the opposite side of the tray. Tell them to get ready for the start – they'll kneel down really low and close to the water. You say 'Ready', then 'Steady' (they will draw breath ready for a really big blow), but when you say 'Go' slap your hand down in the middle of the tray. They get a faceful of water each – serves the little blighters right for being so pushy and competitive!

DOGS AT PARTIES !

Some people like dogs, and some don't. At parties, dogs can, of course, be a real pain. They pinch the ball you're playing with, and jump up and put mud all over your best party frock – just when you'd spent all those hours sewing the sequins on it (only joking). When you think your disco dancing is going particularly well they join in and ruin it by barking and running round and round in stupid circles.

However. Dogs make marvellous waste disposal units. The waste they're particularly good at disposing of is made up of things like:

Sandwich crusts.

The slice of horrible birthday cake you didn't ask for, but got.

Sausage rolls, especially if you're a vegetarian.

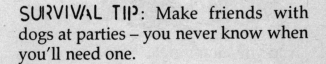

TOTALLY STUFFED

FIT TO BURST

SURVIVAL TIP: Make friends with dogs at parties – you never know when you'll need one.

SURVIVING CHILDREN'S ENTERTAINERS !

Some parents, particularly Mr and Mrs Moneybags (see page 33), think that the only way to entertain children at a party is to employ a *children's entertainer*. This is OK if the children's entertainer is OK, but if he's not it's not. Incidentally children's entertainers are always men. No one is quite sure why this is – perhaps only men are daft enough to be children's entertainers.

The sure sign of a bad children's entertainer is when they start their act with:

'Hello, boys and girls! Are you having a good time?'

And you all mumble 'Yeah.'

And then he says, 'Sorry, I can't quite hear you. ARE YOU HAVING A GOOD TIME?'
And you all go 'Yeah' a bit louder.

And he says, 'Come on now, you can do better than that! Let's hear you, boys and girls.
ARE YOU HAVING A GOOD TIME?'
And you all shout wildly '**YEAH!!!**' – mainly because you want him to shut up and get on with the conjuring tricks, which he then does.

As you now know, a bad children's entertainer is one who thinks that the only way to entertain children is to get them to shout back at you. There is an easy way to cope with this. When he says, 'Hello, boys and girls, are you having a good time?' what you need to do is to shout at the top of your voices:

This will throw him a bit, but he'll press on with, 'Sorry, I didn't hear you, are you having a good time?'

And this time mumble quietly,

This will throw him a good lot more, and he'll ask again, and this time all whisper in polite little voices,

This will throw him completely. He'll forget all his conjuring tricks (which

wouldn't have been any good anyway –
he'd probably have said something
frightful like, 'Observe I have nothing
up my sleeve except my arm and
there's no 'arm in that.' (Groan groan.)
He'll probably rush from the stage and
into the kitchen to look for the gin
bottle (see page 29).

And you can get on with the party.

At any party where friends stay the night it's totally traditional to have a MIDNIGHT FEAST.

WARNING: This can be dangerous.

Midnight Feast Survival Tactics are therefore particularly important. The main difficulty with a midnight feast is that at midnight you're not actually very hungry, and the reason you're not hungry at midnight is that at midnight you're normally fast asleep!

71

So that's two problems
straight away:

1. You're not hungry,

2. You're tired.

There is a third problem:

3. *The food you have saved for a midnight feast is likely (at midnight) to be about as appetising as an old football sock full of stale flour.*

SURVIVAL GUIDE

MIDNIGHT FEASTS !

With the right, simple, tactics you can hold a NEW, IMPROVED, Midnight Feast – and survive!

1. Hold your midnight feast at twenty past nine.

2. Get the menu right.

For example:

The **WRONG** (and usual) Midnight Feast Menu

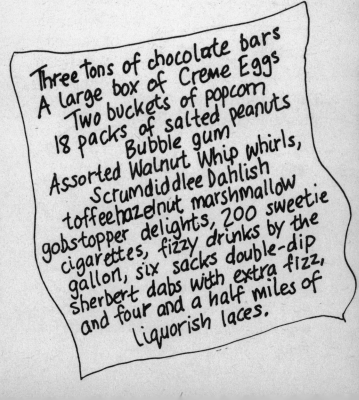

Three tons of chocolate bars
A large box of Creme Eggs
Two buckets of popcorn
18 packs of salted peanuts
Bubble gum
Assorted Walnut Whip whirls,
Scrumdiddlee Dahlish
toffeehazelnut marshmallow
gobstopper delights, 200 sweetie
cigarettes, fizzy drinks by the
gallon, six sacks double-dip
sherbert dabs with extra fizz,
and four and a half miles of
liquorish laces.

YUK! No wonder you seem to spend the first half of the night waiting up for the feast, and the second half sitting on the lavatory wishing you hadn't bothered!

Here is the **RIGHT** Midnight Feast Menu:

1. A sandwich the size of a postage stamp, filled with your favourite filling and with the crusts cut off.

2. An apple or banana – whichever you prefer.

3. Half a tiny after-dinner mint.

4. A small glass of milk.

And, for a really successful new, improved, Midnight Feast, THIS IS WHAT YOU DO:

1. Go to bed at nine o'clock.

2. Giggle and talk for twenty minutes.

3. Eat the feast (see Right menu, opposite).

4. Go to sleep.

5. 'Night-night!

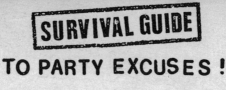

SURVIVAL GUIDE

TO PARTY EXCUSES !

Sometimes, for instance when you get an invitation to a party that you'd rather stand in a ditch full of adders than attend, you need a thoroughbred excuse. Again preparation is the key, so here are a small selection of excuses suitable for most occasions.

I'm sorry I missed your party. I was so thrilled to get the invitation that I took it to be framed, but the framer's shop caught fire, so I didn't know when the party was. Sorry.

I'm sorry I can't come to your party, but I've had an invitation from the Queen to accompany her on a Caribbean cruise on that day, and I don't think I can really let the old girl down.

I'm so sorry that I didn't ask you to my party. The truth is I was fearful that my simple little party could never come up to the expectations of such a debonair, sophisticated and experienced party-goer as you.

I'm sorry, I didn't bring you a present. I'd actually bought you a brand new red Ferrari, but I thought I'd better test it out before I gave it to you just to make sure it was absolutely safe for you — I wouldn't want you to hurt yourself because of me. Anyway, when I'd got it up to about one hundred and sixty miles an hour I hit an oncoming lorry head-on, bounced off the central reservation and disappeared down a cliff and into a steep ravine where the car exploded in a ball of flame. So I don't think you'd want it now.

SURVIVING AT HALLOWEEN !

Some people – particularly Party Poopers (see page 29) – think that Halloween should be banned, and anyone having a Halloween party should be burnt at the stake!

It's certainly true that children of a nervous disposition, for instance children who are scared of the dark, or monsters, or dinner ladies, would be better tucked up in bed with a cup of cocoa and a hot-water bottle, but Halloween parties can be great fun! They can also be just as boring as other parties.

The trouble with most of them is that they're not nearly scary enough. For instance, what's so spooky about Bobbing for Apples?

Here is a new and improved EXTRA SCARY version of BOBBING FOR APPLES

1. Fill a bucket full of water.
2. Float lots of apples in it.
3. Place a large shark in the bottom of the bucket.*
4. Invite guests to get the apples out using only their teeth.
5. STAND WELL BACK AND WATCH THE FUN!

* A stingray or electric eel can be used if no large sharks are available at your local pet-shop.

SURVIVAL THANK-YOU LETTERS
The easy way!

It's often quite a good survival tactic to send the people who asked you to their party a Thank-you Letter.

There are two main reasons why it can be a good idea:

1. If the party was brill and totally fabbo and the best party you've ever been to in your entire life, it's worth telling them this, and flattering them like anything, so that they'll ask you to the next one they organise.

2. In the more likely event that the party was the biggest floppo since the very first firework party – when Guy Fawkes

got caught before he could light the blue touchpaper and retire immediately – it's pretty cool to let them know it, so that next year you'll be spared being sent an invitation and having to invent an excuse for not going.

The trouble with writing thank-you letters is that it's a particularly boring thing to do, and you can never think of anything to say. Here, therefore, in this amazingly useful section of your *Survival Guide to Parties*, is a special **CHOOSE YOUR OWN MISSING WORDS THANK YOU LETTER.**

Dear (their name)

Thank you for asking me to your party YESTERDAY/LAST WEEK/ LAST YEAR/ WHENEVER IT WAS. It was AMAZING/ AMAZINGLY AWFUL/ A DISASTER/ BRILLIANT! In fact it was the BEST/ WORST party I've ever been to (since your last one, that is).

The food was REVOLTING/ WONDERFUL/ OK CONSIDERING THAT YOUR PARENTS DON'T SEEM TO KNOW WHERE THE KITCHEN IS.

Ever since your party I have been ON CLOUD NINE/ON THE LAVATORY.

The games we played were HILARIOUS/ HORRENDOUS, and I must say your MUM/DAD/MUM & DAD is/are VERY ENTERTAINING/ABOUT AS

ENTERTAINING AS A FISH THAT'S BEEN DEAD FOR A WEEK. Having met them I now know why you're such a GREAT KID/GREAT DIP-STICK. Also, your BROTHER/SISTER is a real STAR/SCUMBAG/STAR SCUMBAG.

Oh, and thanks too for the WONDERFUL/MISSING goody-bag. The presents inside it were REALLY TACKY/ABSOLUTELY ACE/NOT THERE. One thing is certain, when I have my next party you WILL/WON'T be getting an invite!

Thanks AGAIN/FOR NOTHING

(your name)

See, that was pretty easy, wasn't it?

SURVIVAL GUIDE

TO THEME PARTIES

Lots of parents these days seem to think it's really cool to have a THEME PARTY. In a misguided attempt to get away from the well-known and well-tested formula of a few games, a good tea and a bit of general messing round, they come up with things like: 'I know, let's take all the children to KING-MAC-BURGER-EXPRESS!' And off you all go to sit on red plastic chairs and eat red plastic mega-whopper-burgers and the smallest greasiest chips ever known to child.

OK if you like that sort of thing, but do you really want a goody-bag with a cap made of paper with swirly cuts in it and KING-MAC-BURGER-EXPRESS written all over it?

Other theme parties include trips to the zoo, adventure playgrounds and parks, and really inventive parents come up with themes like SPACE, HISTORY or THE FLINTSTONES.

SURVIVAL TIP: SPACE is easy. Stick on some pointy ears made of cardboard and say you're Mr Spock.

The main mistake people make about theme parties is thinking that they are anything new. History is full of examples of them, so we look now at:

GREAT THEME PARTIES OF HISTORY

ROMAN TOGA PARTIES

The Romans were brilliant at making stupid straight roads (that all led to Rome), conquering other people, washing with hot water and HAVING PARTIES! Have you ever been to a really good party where the food was so megatastic that after you'd got really full up all you wanted to do was lie down somewhere? Well at Roman parties this happened so often that they actually *started* the meal lying down. WOW!

Also, they wore togas. History books will tell you that togas were long flowing robes wrapped round the body.

This is nonsense. They were actually bedspreads! So, at Roman toga parties you wore your own bedding, lay down, ate and fell asleep. What could be better?

COOL CAVE PARTIES

Even before the Romans, Stone-age man had developed the idea of theme parties. They would start off with some running round – usually chasing giant woolly mammoths with sticks and spears, and then they'd go indoors and do a bit of communal cave painting. (Actually the caves didn't have doors, but since doors hadn't been invented the cavemen didn't realize they hadn't got any. History can be quite confusing at times.)

As they were quite hot after running round – you try dressing up in sheepskins and chasing woolly mammoths – they found the caves nice and cool, which was good. Hence our modern expression - 'Hey, this is a really COOL party!'

SPECIAL NOTE: **THE FIRST RAVE PARTIES**

Later, for bigger, better organised rave parties (not cave parties) Stone-age men built Stonehenge. To keep it really cool they made sure it was very well ventilated. That's why is has no glass in the windows (well, no windows either!).

HOUSE-WARMING PARTIES IN HISTORY

The biggest and best House-Warming Party in History was called the Great Fire of London. Lots of houses got very warm indeed. This is in marked contrast to the first **FIREWORK PARTY** in history because as you know, Guy Fawkes never got the first firework lit. (This can still happen at modern firework parties, usually because it's pouring with rain and your dad drops the matches in a puddle while the fireworks get wet.)

TENPIN BOWLING PARTIES

Lots of parents these days favour tenpin bowling parties. They can be quite fun if you like getting your fingers trapped in small holes in the side of a thing the size of a cannon ball and eventually rolling it down a long corridor and not hitting anything.

SPECIAL NOTE: *There is nothing new about tenpin bowling parties.*

Francis Drake's mum arranged one for him and he had a lot of friends round to the alley in Plymouth. Unfortunately the party was not a great success because the Spanish Armada tried to gatecrash it and Francis had to go off and sink a few ships before he could even get one strike.

TUDOR WIFE-SWAPPING PARTIES

As this book is for dear, sweet, delicate little children, we cannot say much about wife-swapping parties, except that King Henry VIII was always having them. When he got fed up with

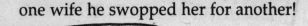

I think I'll have a party. I'd better make a chopping list.

VICTORIAN PARTIES

Victorians had parties but they were never a success because Queen Victoria always refused to be amused. So they all just sat round wearing big black dresses and looking about as jolly as a stuffed turkey on Christmas Eve.

Hello boys and girls. Are you having a good time?

No, we are not amused.

A useful list of key words for the successful party goer… or thrower!

ANORAK

If you ever find yourself at a train-spotting party (bad luck) don't forget to take one. Everyone will be wearing them.

BANDAGES

If you're giving a party it's always wise to have a few ready, in case things get out of hand.

CAKE

Some people think that no party is successful without a really big cake. They are wrong.

DAD

Parties are best when Dad suddenly remembers he's got to go and play golf that afternoon. Dads improve parties by NOT being there!

EMPTY

It's best to go to a party EMPTY…

FULL

…and come back from a party FULL.

GIVING
There's a saying 'to give is better than to receive'. Who are they kidding?

HELICOPTER
If you *really* want to impress your friends, always arrive at parties by helicopter.

ICING
The second most revolting part of a cake. See also **CAKE** (previous page) and **MARZIPAN** (next page).

JAM
An inadequate filling for sandwiches at a party.

KARATE
A usefull skill at any party which is likely to get out of hand. See also **BANDAGES** (previous page).

LAVATORY
It's always sensible to find out where it is *before* the party starts.

MARZIPAN
YUK! The most revolting part of any Cake. See **CAKE** and **ICING** (opposite).
NOSH
One of the most important reasons for going to parties, but don't overdo it.
OVER-EAT
See **NOSH** (above). Don't say we didn't warn you.

POLICE
Also useful if the party gets out of hand.
QUEUE
At parties, this is usually for the Lavatory. See **LAVATORY** (opposite).
RIOT POLICE
Useful if the party gets *really* out of hand!
SICK-BAG
Better to be safe than sorry.

THANK YOU

Saying 'thank you' is a sign of good manners.

UGH!

See **MARZIPAN** (previous page).

VACANT

What the Lavatory at a party never is!
See **LAVATORY** and **QUEUE** (previous page).

WASHING UP

Time to leave the party!

XMAS

That is, Christmas - a good time for parties. (Phew! We didn't think there would be a word beginning with X we could use!)

YULE

Another word for Christmas (Phew yet again!)

ZZZZzzzzzzz

What you do at night after an excellent party!

AUTHOR'S DISCLAIMER

NEITHER THE AUTHOR
NOR THE ILLUSTRATOR
NOR THE PUBLISHER OF
THIS BOOK TAKE ANY
RESPONSIBILITY
WHATSOEVER FOR ANY
FIGHTS, RIOTS OR WORLD
WAR THAT RESULT
DIRECTLY FROM ANY
READER PUTTING ANY
OF ITS CONTENTS INTO
PRACTICE AT ANY
CHILDREN'S PARTIES.

SO THERE.